# INTERMITTENT FASTING

## FOR WOMEN OVER 50

### THE FASTEST AND MOST SUSTAINABLE 16-8 OR 18-6 DIET METHOD TO LOSE FAT AND BE IN BEAUTIFUL SHAPE

### +45 RECIPES WITH PICTURES

*Georgia Greathearted*

# Contents

# INTRODUCTION

Researchers have been studying intermittent fasting for decades.

Study findings are sometimes contradictory and inconclusive. However, the research on intermittent fasting, including 16:8 fasting, indicates that it may provide benefit as weight loss and fat loss.

Eating during a set period can help people reduce the number of calories that they consume. It may also help boost metabolism.

Intermittent fasting is a simple lifestyle change that can help in reversing several chronic illnesses. It is an age-old practice that humankind had been practicing for hundreds of thousands of years. Our bodies have evolved on this system, and hence they work the best with it.

The simple fasting method and eating at certain intervals can help your systems recover from years of abuse that you have also been subjecting them. It is a comprehensive way to lose way through the correct method, which would also help ease the burden from your body.

Intermittent fasting creates a system where your body can respond better to various changes. It also helps your organization in beginning the process of autophagy that can even start the self-healing process.

Two fundamental concepts that you will hear in this context are:

- Ketosis
- Autophagy

## Ketosis

Ketosis is the process of burning fat for energy. Most people are trying to lose weight, fail to get any success or gain more than they had ever suffered. This situation happens because they hadn't lost any weight in reality. Most of the time, the lost weight is just the water weight that their body loses to adjust to the current energy crisis.

Your body would have to begin the process of ketosis to lose weight. Intermittent fasting can help you at the beginning of this process fast. Aided with a proper nutrition plan, you can expect ketosis to begin rapidly, and not only will your weight go down, but you will also experience fat-burning from your abdomen, thighs, and hips.

## Autophagy

You might have come across another term recently if you have been following the health news closely. It is a process of self-cleaning that your body is capable of carrying out under the right conditions. A study on this subject has helped a Japanese researcher win the 2016 Nobel Prize in medicine. This process can unlock the secret of longevity, health, and cure from some of the most untreatable conditions. The research on this subject has brought to light that the body can start purging all the inefficient processes, pathogens, and useless material inside the authority to make it more energy-efficient under correct fasting conditions. This process can help in healing from several illnesses, and it also has potent anti-ageing effects.

Both these processes, combined with intermittent fasting, can help you fight most of the chronic illnesses in your body to a great extent.

Intermittent fasting is a positive lifestyle change that can help you reverse the negative impact of chronic illnesses, and you can expect to live your future life in better health.

Some of the most adamant health issues that we keep struggling with for most of our lives but see no end to them. Intermittent fasting can also help you in fighting even those issues.

One such problem is obesity. Increasing weight and waistline is among the chief concerns of women of all age groups. However, it becomes a primary health concern of women in their 50s as it also starts affecting their overall health.

The first advice health care professionals give to overweight women is to control their weight to stay healthy. However, that's easy said than done.

Weight is adamant, and especially the belly fat refuses to go. Women, throughout their lives, try numerous methods but to no avail. Getting rid of weight is a big problem, but preventing weight relapse is an even bigger problem once you have lost some weight.

Statistics show that more than 85% of women who had lost weight eventually regained more than they had lost.

Intermittent fasting can help you in getting freedom from this vicious cycle of gaining and losing weight. You can successfully lose weight and easily maintain it with the help of an intermittent fasting lifestyle.

# Chapter 1

## METHODS AND BENEFITS
## FOR WOMEN OVER 50

Women over 50 can do anything to lose weight at their age, precisely because it becomes complicated to do so with advancing years.

There are many reasons why it is impossible to lose weight, but the main culprit is often a slowed-down metabolism. It is the lean body mass that allows us to lose weight, i.e. the muscles. The more strength you have, the faster your metabolism is. But as we get older, our muscles decrease in thickness, and we often lose them because we also do less sporting activity.

The result of all this is stubborn fat that doesn't seem to want to leave us.

Intermittent fasting is very easy to follow because it does not restrict our food choices too much and has many health benefits at the same time. Perhaps it is also for these reasons that it has become a popular method.

Research shows that fasting can improve metabolism and mental health and even prevent certain cancers; it can also ward off certain muscle, nerve, and joint disorders, affecting women over 50.

There are several IF variants to choose from, as you select a period to deprive yourself of food.

You can choose the variant that suits your working hours, your lifestyle, and your well-being.

Obviously, before embarking on any diet or changing your eating plan, it is always best to consult your doctor.

The most popular method is called the "Daily Method". It is also the most sustainable method.

This eating plan follows the 16/8 or 18/6 rule. It means that you can only eat food for 6 to 8 hours during the day while you have to fast the rest of the time.

When you can eat, the meals you take must be healthy, so you must eliminate fried food, excessive condiments, and fat.

There are also other variations to implementing an intermittent diet. People who find it difficult to follow a diet could, for example, start with the more tolerable 12/12 method. This method consists of eating for 12 hours and then fasting for 12 hours. Once you have got used to this, you can move on to the more rigorous schedule of 16/8 or 18/06.

A more challenging method is the 5:2. In this case, you do not plan to eat in a specific time frame but determine when you can eat and the days when you eat very few calories or even fast.

Specifically, you usually eat for five days, and the next two days, you eat tiny calories.

This approach consists of eating ordinary, healthy meals for five days of the week and then limiting yourself to 500-600 calories for the next two days.

It is not clear whether it is more beneficial to eat all your calories in one meal or to spread them out for the day, so do what works for you.

Another method is the alternate day method.

With this method, you usually eat one day and eat much less or nothing at all the next day. The only thing you need to know is the calories you eat when you usually eat. Suppose you typically eat meals that total 1800 calories, then on the day after the diet. In that case, you should eat meals that add up to only 25% of your daily calorie intake, so if you follow this example calculation, the calories you will feast on your diet day will be 450, which is 25% of 1800.

There is also the 24-hour method, where you eat for 24 hours and fast for the other 24.

This method is effective if done one day a week or two at the most. It is also better to fast from breakfast to breakfast or from lunch to lunch and is usually done only once or maximum twice a week.

This situation is a method that is not suitable for everyone, and you must check whether it is ideal for you. It is a method that you should be implemented with extreme caution because when you are fasting, it will make you feel very irritable, tired and you may also have severe headaches.

Intermittent fasting has many benefits, especially for women, and not just for weight loss.

Research shows that fasting can improve your metabolism, mental health and possibly prevent some cancers.

It can also ward off certain muscle, nerve, and joint disorders, affecting women over 50.

## Musculoskeletal health

This effect includes conditions like osteoporosis, arthritis, and lower back pain. Fasting has shown to promote hormone secretion from the thyroid. This situation can promote bone health and help prevent bone fractures.

## Metabolic health

Some women go through menopause in their 50s. Menopause can cause changes in your body that increase belly fat, insulin, and glucose. Fasting can help you decrease your blood pressure, cholesterol, and belly fat, improving insulin sensitivity. Fasting can also keep your metabolism on track as you age.

## Mental health

Fasting has shown to promote mental health. It may reduce anxiety, depression, and the emotional roller coaster that can go hand-in-hand with menopause. Fasting has also proved to improve self-esteem and reduce stress.

Other proven benefits of IF include:

- Improved memory
- Tissue health
- Physical performance
- Heart health

The fasting diet is a practice that dates back to ancient times and, in some cultures, is still practiced regularly.

Who Shouldn't Try Intermittent Fasting?

Intermittent fasting isn't for everyone.

You should always check with your doctor before trying a new diet, even one that's proven to be beneficial.

The following groups of people should avoid IF:

- People who suffer from diabetes or other blood sugar problems
- Children under the age of 18
- People with a history of eating disorders
- Pregnant and breastfeeding women

# Chapter 2

## A GUIDE TO 16:8 METHOD

Because of the ease with which it can follow, consider the intermittent fasting 16:8 method.

As I explained in the previous chapter, it is a form of time-limited fasting that consists of consuming food during an 8-hour window and avoiding food, or fasting, for the remaining 16 hours each day.

Some people believe that this method supports the body's circadian rhythm, which is its internal clock.

Most people who follow the 16:8 plans abstain from food at night and for part of the morning and evening. They tend to consume their daily calories during the middle of the day.

There are no restrictions on the types or amounts of food that a person can eat during the 8-hour window. This flexibility makes the plan relatively easy to follow.

Suggested benefits of the 16:8 plan include weight loss and fat loss and the prevention of type 2 diabetes and other obesity-associated conditions.

The easiest way to follow the 16:8 diet is to choose a 16-hour fasting window that includes the time that a person spends sleeping.

Some experts advise finishing food consumption in the early evening, as metabolism slows down after this time. However, this is not feasible for everyone.

Some people may not be able to consume their evening meal until 7 p.m. or later. Even so, it is best to avoid food for 2–3 hours before bed.

People may choose one of the following 8-hour eating windows:

   9 a.m. to 5 p.m.

- 10 a.m. to 6 p.m.
- Noon to 8 p.m.

Within this timeframe, people can eat their meals and snacks at convenient times. Eating at a specific time every day is essential to prevent blood sugar peaks and dips and avoid excessive hunger.

Some people may need to experiment to find the best eating window and mealtimes for their lifestyle.

While the 16:8 intermittent fasting plan does not specify which foods to eat and avoid, it is beneficial to focus on healthful eating and to limit or avoiding junk foods. The consumption of too much unhealthful food may cause weight gain and contribute to disease.

A balanced diet focuses primarily on: fruits and vegetables, which can be fresh, frozen, or canned (in water)

- whole grains, including quinoa, brown rice, oats, and barley
- lean protein sources, such as poultry, fish, beans, lentils, tofu, nuts, seeds, low fat cottage cheese, and eggs
- healthful fats from fatty fish, olives, olive oil, coconuts, avocados, nuts, and seeds
- Fruits, vegetables, and whole grains are high in fiber, so they can help keep a person feeling full and satisfied. Healthful fats and proteins can also contribute to satiety.

## Welcome Food

Here following there are some suggested foods to eat during the diet:

Eggs: make sure you eat the yolk because this contains vitamins and protein!

Leafy greens: we're talking about things like spinach, collards, kale, and Swiss chards, to name a few, and these packed with fibre and low in calories too

Oily and fatty fish, such as salmon: salmon is a fish that will keep you feeling full, but it's also high in omega-three fatty acids, which are ideal for boosting brain health, reducing inflammation, and generally helping with weight loss too. If salmon isn't your bag, try mackerel, trout, herring, and sardines instead.

Cruciferous vegetables: in this case, you need to look toward Brussels sprouts, broccoli, cabbage, and cauliflower. Again, these types of vegetables contain a high fibre amount that helps you feel fuller for longer and have cancer-fighting attributes.

Lean meats: stick to beef and chicken for the best options, but make sure that you go for the leanest cuts possible. You'll get a good protein boost here, but you can also make all manner of delicious dishes with both types of meat!

Boiled potatoes: you might think that potatoes are harmful to you, and in most cases, they are, especially if you fry them, but boiled potatoes are a good choice, especially if you lack potassium. They are also very filling.

Tuna: This is a different type of fish from the oily fish we mentioned earlier, and it's deficient in fat but high in protein. Go for tuna, which is canned contain water and not oil, for the healthiest option. Pile it onto a jacket potato for a delicious and healthy meal!

Beans and other types of legumes: These are the staple of any healthy diet and are super filling. We're talking about kidney beans, lentils, black beans here, and they're high in fibre and protein.

Cottage cheese: If you're a cheese fan, there's no reason to deny yourself, but most cheeses are pretty high in fat. In that case, why not opt for cottage cheese instead? This effect is high in protein and quite filling but low in calories.

Avocados: the fad food of the moment is very healthy and great for boosting your brainpower! Mash it up on some toast for a great breakfast packed with potassium and plenty of fibre.

Nuts: instead of snacking on chocolate and crisps, why not snack on nuts? You'll get incredible amounts of healthy fats, as well as fibre and protein, and they're filling too. Don't eat too many, however, as they can be high in calories if you overindulge.

Whole grains: everyone knows that whole grains are packed with fibre and therefore keep you fuller for longer, so this is the ideal choice for anyone who is trying intermittent fasting. Try quinoa, brown rice, and oats to get you started.

Fruits: not all fruits are healthy, but they're certainly a better option than chocolate and crisps! You'll also get a plethora of different vitamins and minerals, as well as a boost of antioxidants into your diet - ideal for your immune system.

Seeds: again, just like nuts, seeds make a great snack, and they can sprinkle them on many foods, such as yoghurt and porridge. Try chia seeds for a high fibre treat whilst being low calorie at the same time.

Coconut oil and extra virgin olive oil: you will undoubtedly have heard of the wonders of coconut oil, and this is a very healthy oil you can try cooking. Coconut oil is up of medium-chain triglycerides, and whilst you might panic at the word triglycerides, these are the beneficial type! If you want to go for something deficient in calories, however, then you can't beat extra virgin olive oil.

Yoghurt: perfect for a gut health boost; yoghurt is your friend because it will keep you full, and it also has probiotic content, provided you go for products that say 'live and active cultures on the pot. Avoid the overly sugary yoghurt treats, and anything which says 'low fat' generally isn't as positive as it sounds!

## Foods to Avoid

Sugary foods may curb your appetite, but they won't do anything good for your body in the long run. Steer clear for your future ease.

Highly GMO foods are also things to avoid when you're working through your fast. They can offset the actual nutrition provided by other foods in your diet.

## Drinks to Take

Beverages can play a role in satiety for those following the 16:8 intermittent fasting diet. Drinking water regularly throughout the day can help reduce calorie intake because people often mistake thirst for hunger.

## Tips

The 16:8 diet plan permits consuming calorie-free drinks — such as water and unsweetened tea and coffee — during the 16-hour fasting window. It is important to consume fluids regularly to avoid dehydration.

You are allowed to take drinks while fasting. Go for drinks that are nutritious because they are suitable for the body. Some of the drinks that you can take are listed below;

Water with fruit or veggie slices will provide nourishment and flavour for those times when you're fasting and need a little extra boost!

Probiotic drinks like kombucha or kefir will work to heal your gut and tide you over till the next eating window.

Black coffee will become your new best friend but be sure not to add cream and sugar! They detract from the excellent work coffee can do for your body during IF.

Teas of any kind are soothing and healing for various elements of the body, mind, and soul. Once again, be sure to omit the cream and sugar!

Chilled or heated broths made from vegetables, bone, or animals can sustain one's energy during times of fast, too.

Apple Cider Vinegar shots are great for the tummy and for healing overall! Hippocrates' remedy for any ailment included this and a healthy fasting regimen occasionally, so you're sure to succeed with this trick.

Water with salt can provide electrolytes, hydration, and brief sustenance for anyone whose stomachs won't stop grumbling.

Fresh-pressed juices are always great for the body, mind, and soul, and in times of IF, they can sustain one's energy and mood during day-long fast periods.

Wheatgrass shots are just as healthy as ACV shots, with a whole other subset of benefits. To awaken your body and give a jolt to your system, try these on for size.

Coconut water is more hydrating than standard water, and it's full of additional nutrients, too!

Try this alternative if you need some enhancement to your normal water.

People may find it easier to stick to the 16:8 diets when they follow these tips:

- drinking cinnamon herbal tea during the fasting period, as it may suppress the appetite;
- consuming water regularly throughout the day;
- watching less television to reduce exposure to images of food, which may stimulate a sense of hunger;
- exercising just before or during the eating window, as exercise can trigger hunger;
- practicing mindful eating when consuming meals;
- Try meditation during the fasting period to allow hunger pangs to pass.

Here you will find 45 healthy recipes that you can enjoy at mealtimes during your diet.

# Chapter 3

## BREAKFAST

# 01_PULLED PORK BREAKFAST HASH

**Preparation Time**: 5 minutes
**Cooking Time:** 10 minutes
**Servings:** 2

## Nutrition:

Calories: 355; Carbohydrates: 7g  Protein: 21g  Fat: 22g  Sugar: 1.6g, Sodium: 307mg, Fiber: 0.7g

## INGREDIENTS

- **2** TABLESPOONS OF OLIVE OIL
- **1** TURNIP, FINELY CHOPPED
- **2** TABLESPOONS OF RED ONION, FINELY CHOPPED
- **½** CUP OF COOKED PULLED PORK
- **2** LARGE ORGANIC EGGS
- **1** CUP OF KALE, STEMMED AND ROUGHLY CHOPPED
- **4** BRUSSEL SPROUTS, HALVED
- **1** TEASPOON OF SMOKED PAPRIKA
- **1** TEASPOON OF FINE SEA SALT
- **1** TEASPOON OF FRESHLY CRACKED BLACK PEPPER

## DIRECTIONS

1) Press the "Sauté" function on your Instant Pot and add the olive oil, turnips and onions. Cook until the vegetables have softened, stirring occasionally.

2) Add the seasoning and remaining vegetables. Sauté for another 2 minutes, stirring occasionally.

3) Add the pulled pork and cook for another 2 minutes.

4) Remove all the contents and transfer to an oven-proof dish that fits inside your Instant Pot.

5) Create two separate divots into the dish and crack the eggs. Cover with aluminum foil.

6) Add 2 cups of water and a trivet to your Instant Pot. Lock the lid and cook at high pressure for 3 minutes.

7) When the cooking is done, naturally release the pressure and remove the lid. Check if the eggs are set.

8) Serve and enjoy!

# 02_BUTTERY DATE PANCAKES

**Preparation Time:** 10 minutes
**Cooking Time:** 10 minutes
**Servings:** 3

## INGREDIENTS

- **1/4** CUP ALMOND FLOUR
- **3** EGGS, BEATEN
- **1** TEASPOON OLIVE OIL
- **6** DATES, PITTED
- **1** TABLESPOON ALMOND BUTTER
- **1** TEASPOON VANILLA EXTRACT
- **1/2** TEASPOON GROUND CINNAMON

## DIRECTIONS

1) Stir the eggs in a bowl make them fluffy.
2) Wash the dates and cut them in half.
3) Discard the seeds and mash them finely.
4) Melt the almond butter and add to the eggs.
5) Add the almond flour, olive oil, and cinnamon.
6) Mix well and add the vanilla extract.
7) Mix into a smooth batter.
8) Add the date paste and mix well.
9) In a pan, heat the butter over medium heat.
10) Add the batter using a spoon and fry them golden brown from both sides.
11) Repeat with all the batter.
12) Serve with melted butter on top.

## Nutrition:

Calories 281
Fat 20g
Protein 10.5g
Carbohydrates 4.5g

# 03_Low Carb Pancake Crepes

**Preparation Time:** 10 minutes
**Cooking Time:** 10 minutes
**Servings: 2**

## Nutrition:

Calories 241, Fats 21.8 g , Carbohydrates 2.4g, Proteins 9.6 g

## INGREDIENTS

- **3** OUNCES CREAM CHEESE
- **1** TSP. GROUND CINNAMON
- **1** TBSP HONEY
- **1** TSP. GROUND CARDAMOM
- **1** TSP. BUTTER
- **2** EGG, BEATEN

## DIRECTIONS

1) In a bowl, whisk the eggs finely.
2) Beat the cream cheese in a different bowl until it becomes soft.
3) Add the egg mixture to the softened cream cheese and mix well until there are no lumps left.
4) Add cinnamon, cardamom, and honey to it. Mix well. The batter would be runnier than of pancake batter.
5) In a pan, add the butter and heat over medium heat.
6) Add the batter using a scooper; that way, all the size of the crepes would be the same.
7) Fry them golden brown on both sides.
8) Repeat the process with the rest of the batter.
9) Drizzle some honey on top and enjoy.

# 04_MORNING MEATLOAF

**Preparation Time:** 10 minutes
**Cooking Time:** 20 minutes
**Servings: 6**

## Nutrition:

Calories 592, Carbohydrates 2.5g, Proteins 11g , Fats 49.5g

## INGREDIENTS

- **1 ½** POUND OF BREAKFAST SAUSAGE
- **6** LARGE ORGANIC EGGS
- **2** TABLESPOONS OF UNSWEETENED NON-DAIRY MILK
- **1** SMALL ONION, FINELY CHOPPED
- **2** MEDIUM GARLIC CLOVES, PEELED AND MINCED
- **4**-OUNCES OF CREAM CHEESE SOFTENED AND CUBED
- **1** CUP OF SHREDDED CHEDDAR CHEESE
- **2** TABLESPOONS OF SCALLIONS, CHOPPED
- **1** CUP OF WATER

## DIRECTIONS

1) Add all the ingredients apart from water in a large bowl. Stir until well combined.

2) Form the sausage mixture into a meatloaf and wrap with a sheet of aluminum foil. Ensure that the meatloaf fits inside your Instant Pot. If not, remove parts of the mixture and reserve for future use.

3) Once you wrap the meatloaf into a packet, add 1 cup of water and a trivet to your Instant Pot. Put the meatloaf on the trivet's top.

4) Cover and cook for 25 minutes on high pressure. When done, quickly release the pressure. Carefully remove the lid.

5) Unwrap the meatloaf and check if the meatloaf is done. Serve and enjoy!

# 05_SAVORY BREAKFAST MUFFINS

**Preparation Time:** 10 minutes
**Cooking Time:** 35 minutes
**Servings: 6**

## Nutrition:

Calories 388, Fat 25.8g, Carbohydrate 8.6g, Proteins 25.3g

## INGREDIENTS

- **8** EGGS
- **1** CUP SHREDDED CHEESE
- SALT AND PEPPER TO TASTE
- **½** TSP. BAKING POWDER
- **¼** CUP DICED ONION
- **2/3** CUP COCONUT FLOUR
- **1 ½** CUP SPINACH
- **¼** CUP FULL FAT COCONUT MILK
- **1** TBSP BASIL, CHOPPED
- **½** CUP COOKED CHICKEN, DICED FINELY

## DIRECTIONS

1) Preheat the oven to 375-degree F.

2) Use butter or oil to grease your muffin tray or you can use muffin paper liners.

3) In a large mixing bowl, whisk the eggs.

4) Add in the coconut milk and mix again.

5) Gradually shift in the coconut flour with baking powder salt.

6) Add in the cooked chicken, onion, spinach, basil, and combine well.

7) Add the cheese and mix again.

8) Pour the mixture onto your muffin liners.

9) Bake for about 25 minutes.

10)     Serve at room temperature.

# 06_CHIA SEED BANANA BLUEBERRY DELIGHT

**Preparation Time:** 30 minutes
**Cooking Time:** 0 minutes
**Servings: 2**

## Nutrition:

Calories 260, Fats 26.6g, Carbohydrates 17.4g , Protein 4.1g

## INGREDIENTS

- **1 CUP YOGURT**
- **½ CUP BLUEBERRIES**
- **1/2 TSP. SALT**
- **1/2 TSP. CINNAMON**
- **1 BANANA**
- **1 TSP. VANILLA EXTRACT**
- **1/4 CUP CHIA SEEDS**

## DIRECTIONS

1) Discard the skin of the banana.

2) Cut into semi-thick circles.

3) You can mash them or keep them as a whole if you like to bite into your fruits.

4) Clean the blueberries properly and rinse well.

5) Soak the chia seeds in water for 30 minutes or longer.

6) Drain the chia seeds and transfer them into a bowl.

7) Add the yogurt and mix well.

8) Add the salt, cinnamon, and vanilla and mix again.

9) Now fold in the bananas and blueberries gently.

10) If you want to add dried fruit or nuts, add it and then serve immediately.

11) This is best served cold.

# 07_Choco Chip Whey Waffles

**Preparation Time:** 10 minutes
**Cooking Time:** 6 minutes
**Servings:** 2

## Ingredients

- **2** TABLESPOONS ORGANIC COCONUT OIL
- **2** TABLESPOONS COCONUT SUGAR
- **4** TABLESPOONS CHOCOLATE WHEY PROTEIN POWDER
- **⅓** CUP ALMOND FLOUR
- **A** PINCH OF SALT
- **½** TEASPOON BAKING POWDER
- **2**-PCS EGGS

## Directions

1) Mix all the ingredients in the blender to obtain a homogenous paste.

2) Preheat your waffle iron. Pour the waffle dough in the iron and cook each waffle for 3 minutes.

## Nutrition:

Calories: 423,

Fat: 32.8g,

Protein: 26.5g,

Total Carbohydrates: 8.3g,

Dietary Fiber: 2.9g

# 08_WHOLESOME MUSHROOM AND CAULIFLOWER RISOTTO

**Preparation Time:** 15 minutes
**Cooking Time:** 10 minutes
**Servings:** 4

## INGREDIENTS

- **1** MEDIUM CAULIFLOWER HEAD, CUT INTO FLORETS
- **1** POUND OF SHIITAKE MUSHROOMS, SLICED
- **3** MEDIUM GARLIC CLOVES, PEELED AND MINCED
- **2** TABLESPOONS OF COCONUT AMINOS
- **1** CUP OF HOMEMADE LOW-SODIUM CHICKEN STOCK
- **1** CUP OF FULL-FAT COCONUT MILK
- **1** TABLESPOON OF COCONUT OIL, MELTED
- **1** SMALL ONION, FINELY CHOPPED
- **2** TABLESPOONS OF ALMOND FLOUR
- **¼** CUP OF NUTRITIONAL YEAST

## DIRECTIONS

1) Press the "Sauté" function on your Instant Pot and add the coconut oil.

2) Once hot, add the onions, mushrooms and garlic. Sauté for 5 minutes or until softened, stirring occasionally.

3) Add the remaining ingredients except for the almond flour. Lock the lid and cook at high pressure for 2 minutes.

4) When the cooking is done, naturally release the pressure and remove the lid.

5) Sprinkle the almond flour over the risotto and stir to thicken. Serve and enjoy!

## Nutrition:

Calories: 230;  Carbohydrates: 8g, Protein: 7.5g

Fat: 18g  Sugar: 2.1g, Sodium: 432mg  Fiber: 1.2g

# CHAPTER 4
# Lunch

# 09_PRAWN "ARRABBIATA"

**Preparation Time:** 10 minutes
**Cooking Time:** 40 minutes
**Servings: 1**

## INGREDIENTS:

- RAW OR COOKED PRAWNS (IDEALLY KING PRAWNS)
- 1.5 OUNCE OF BUCKWHEAT PASTA
- 1 TABLESPOON EXTRA-VIRGIN OLIVE OIL
- FOR ARRABBIATA SAUCE
- RED ONION, FINELY CHOPPED
- 1 GARLIC CLOVE, FINELY CHOPPED
- 1.2-OUNCE CELERY, FINELY CHOPPED
- 1 BIRD'S EYE CHILI, FINELY CHOPPED
- 1 TEASPOON DRIED MIXED HERBS
- 1 TEASPOON EXTRA-VIRGIN OLIVE OIL
- 2 TABLESPOONS. WHITE WINE (OPTIONAL)
- 14-OUNCE TINNED CHOPPED TOMATOES
- 1 TABLESPOON. CHOPPED PARSLEY

## DIRECTIONS:

1) Firstly, you fry the onion, garlic, celery and chili over medium-low heat and dry herbs in the oil for 1–2 minutes. Switch the flame to medium, then add the wine and cook 1 minute. Add the tomatoes and leave the sauce to cook for 20-30 minutes over medium-low heat until it has a nice rich consistency. If you feel the sauce becomes too thick, add some water.

2) While the sauce is cooking, boil a pan of water, and cook the pasta as directed by the packet. Drain, toss with the olive oil when cooked to your liking, and keep in the pan until needed.

3) Add the raw prawns to the sauce and cook for another 3–4 minutes until they have turned pink and opaque, then attach the parsley and serve. If you use cooked prawns add the parsley, bring the sauce to the boil and eat.

4) Add the cooked pasta to the sauce, blend well, and then serve gently.

## Nutrition:

Calories: 185, Fat 30g, Protein 56g, Carbohydrate 45g, Cholesterol 230mg, Sugar 0g

# 10_ZUPPA TOSCANA WITH CAULIFLOWER

**Preparation Time:** 5 minutes
**Cooking Time:** 25 minutes
**Servings:** 4

## INGREDIENTS:

- 1-POUND GROUND ITALIAN SAUSAGE
- 6 CUPS HOMEMADE LOW-SODIUM CHICKEN STOCK
- 2 CUPS CAULIFLOWER FLORETS - 1 ONION, FINELY CHOPPED
- 1 CUP KALE, STEMMED AND ROUGHLY CHOPPED
- 1 (14.5-OUNCE) CAN OF FULL-FAT COCONUT MILK
- ¼ TEASPOON SEA SALT
- ¼ TEASPOON FRESHLY CRACKED BLACK PEPPER

## DIRECTIONS:

1) On the Instant Pot, press "Sauté" and add the ground Italian sausage. Cook until brown, stirring occasionally and breaking up the meat with a wooden spoon.

2) Add the remaining ingredients except for the kale and coconut milk and stir until well combined.

3) Cover and cook for 10 minutes on high pressure. When done, release the pressure naturally and remove the lid. Stir in the kale and coconut milk. Cover and sit for 5 minutes or until the kale has wilted. Serve and enjoy!

## Nutrition:

Calories 653, Carbohydrates 8g, Protein 26g, Fat 4g

# 11_Garlic Butter Beef Steak

**Preparation Time:** 5 minutes
**Cooking Time:** 15 minutes
**Servings: 2**

## Nutrition:

Calories 337

Carbohydrates 2.5g

Protein 34.5g

Fat 18.7g

## Ingredients:

- **1-POUND BEEF SIRLOIN STEAKS**
- **½ CUP RED WINE**
- **4 TABLESPOONS UNSALTED BUTTER**
- **2 TABLESPOONS FRESH PARSLEY, FINELY CHOPPED**
- **4 MEDIUM GARLIC CLOVES, PEELED AND MINCED**
- **FINE SEA SALT AND FRESHLY CRACKED BLACK PEPPER**

## Directions:

1) Season the beef steaks with sea salt and freshly cracked black pepper.

2) On the Instant Pot, press "Sauté" and add the butter. Once melted, add the beef steaks and sear for 2 minutes per side or until brown.

3) Pour in the red wine and fresh parsley. Cover and cook for 12 minutes on high pressure. When done, release the pressure naturally and carefully remove the lid.

4) Top the steak with the butter sauce. Serve and enjoy!

# 12_Instant Pot Teriyaki Chicken

**Preparation Time:** 5 minutes
**Cooking Time:** 35 minutes
**Servings:** 4

## Nutrition:

Calories 259, Carbohydrates 33.1g, Protein 24.3g, Fats 2.3g

## INGREDIENTS

- **1/2** CUP SOY SAUCE
- **1/2** CUP WATER
- **1/2** CUP BROWN SUGAR
- **2** TBSPS. RICE WINE VINEGAR
- **1** TBSP. MIRIN (JAPANESE SWEET WINE)
- **1** TBSP. SAKE
- **1** TBSP. MINCED GARLIC
- **1** DASH FRESHLY CRACKED BLACK PEPPER
- **1** LB. SKINLESS, BONELESS CHICKEN

## DIRECTIONS:

1) Combine soy sauce, brown sugar, water, rice wine vinegar, sake, mirin, pepper, and garlic in a bowl to prepare the sauce.

2) Put chicken in an electric pressure cooker (such as Instant Pot(R)). Pour the sauce over.

3) Close lid and lock. Set to Meat function, with the timer on to 12 minutes. Give 10-15 minutes for pressure to build.

4) Gently release pressure with the quick-release method according to manufacturer's instructions, for 5 minutes. Remove lid. Insert the instant read thermometer into the middle of the chicken and make sure to reach at least 165°F (74°C). If not hot enough, cook for 2-4 more minutes.

5) Take chicken out from the cooker. Shred or cut up. Mix with sauce from the pot.

# 13_PORK CARNITAS

**Preparation Time**: 20 minutes
**Cooking Time:** 1 hour
**Servings: 4**

## Nutrition:

Calories 170, Carbohydrates 2g, Protein 4g, Fat 8g

## INGREDIENTS:

- **6** MEDIUM GARLIC CLOVES, MINCED
- **2** TEASPOONS GROUND CUMIN
- **1** TEASPOON SMOKED PAPRIKA
- **3** CHIPOTLE PEPPERS IN ADOBO SAUCE, MINCED
- **1** TEASPOON DRIED OREGANO
- **2** BAY LEAVES
- **1** CUP HOMEMADE LOW-SODIUM CHICKEN BROTH
- FINE SEA SALT AND FRESHLY CRACKED BLACK PEPPER
- **2** TABLESPOONS OF OLIVE OIL
- **2 ½** POUNDS BONELESS PORK SHOULDER, CUT INTO **4** LARGE PIECES

## DIRECTIONS:

1) Season the pork shoulder with sea salt, black pepper, ground cumin, dried oregano, and smoked paprika.
2) On the Instant Pot, press "Sauté" and add the olive oil.
3) Once hot, add the pork pieces and sear for 4 minutes per side or until brown.
4) Add the remaining ingredients inside your Instant Pot. Cover and cook for 80 minutes on high pressure. When done, quick release the pressure and remove the lid.
5) Carefully shred the pork using two forks and continue to stir until well coated with the liquid.
6) Remove the bay leave and adjust the seasoning if necessary. Serve and enjoy!

# 14_Instant Pot Meatballs

**Preparation Time:** 5 minutes
**Cooking Time:** 30 minutes
**Servings: 4**

## Nutrition:

Calories 243, Carbohydrates 3g, Protein 19g, Fats 4g

## INGREDIENTS:

- **2** POUNDS GROUND MEAT
- **1** SMALL ONION, FINELY CHOPPED
- **4** MEDIUM GARLIC CLOVES, PEELED AND MINCED
- **2** LARGE ORGANIC EGGS
- **4** TABLESPOONS RANCH DRESSING
- **4** TABLESPOONS ALMOND FLOUR
- **2** TABLESPOONS FRESH PARSLEY, FINELY CHOPPED
- **2** TABLESPOONS WORCESTERSHIRE SAUCE
- **1** CUP HOT SAUCE
- **½** CUP UNSALTED BUTTER
- **½** CUP WATER

## DIRECTIONS:

1) In a large bowl, add the garlic, eggs, ground meat, onion, ranch dressing, parsley, and almond flour. Mix until well combined.

2) Preheat your broiler. Form balls from the mixture and put on a baking sheet. Broil for 10 minutes or until brown. Remove and set aside.

3) On the Instant Pot, press "Sauté" and add the butter. Once melted, stir in the hot sauce, Worcestershire sauce and water.

4) Stir in the chicken meatballs and cover. Cook for 15 minutes on high pressure. Release the pressure naturally for 10 minutes, then quick release the remaining pressure. Carefully remove the lid. Serve and enjoy!

# 15_TERIYAKI SALMON

**Preparation Time:** 15 minutes
**Cooking Time:** 5 minutes
**Servings: 2**

## Nutrition:

Calories 93, Carbohydrates 3g, Protein 13g, Fats 4g

## INGREDIENTS:

- **3** TBSPS. LIME JUICE
- **2** TBSPS. OLIVE OIL
- **2** TBSPS. REDUCED-SODIUM TERIYAKI SAUCE
- **1** TBSP. BALSAMIC VINEGAR
- **1** TBSP. DIJON MUSTARD
- **1** TSP. GARLIC POWDER
- **6** DROPS HOT PEPPER SAUCE
- **6** UNCOOKED JUMBO SALMON

## DIRECTIONS:

1) Mix together the all ingredients except the salmon in a big zip lock plastic bag then put in the shrimp. Seal the zip lock bag and turn to coat the salmon. Keep in the fridge for an hour and occasionally turn.

2) Drain the marinated salmon and discard marinade. Broil the salmon 4 inches from heat for 3 to 4 minutes per side or until the salmon turn pink in color.

# 16_CREAMY LAMB KORMA

**Preparation Time:** 5 minutes
**Cooking Time:** 35 minutes
**Servings:** 4

## Nutrition:

Calories 280, Carbohydrates 5g, Protein 26g , Fat: 25g

## INGREDIENTS:

- 1-POUND LAMB STEAK, CUT INTO 1-INCH PIECES
- 1 TABLESPOON EXTRA-VIRGIN OLIVE OIL
- 1 MEDIUM ONION, FINELY CHOPPED
- 1-INCH PIECE GINGER, PEELED AND MINCED
- 6 MEDIUM GARLIC CLOVES, PEELED AND MINCED
- 2 TABLESPOONS TOMATO PASTE
- ½ CUP COCONUT MILK OR PLAIN YOGURT
- ¾ CUPS WATER
- 3 TEASPOONS GARAM MASALA
- ½ TEASPOON TURMERIC POWDER
- 1 TEASPOON SMOKED OR REGULAR PAPRIKA
- ½ TEASPOON CARDAMOM POWDER
- ¼ TEASPOON SEA SALT
- ¼ TEASPOON FRESHLY CRACKED BLACK PEPPER

## DIRECTIONS:

1) On the Instant Pot, press "Sauté" and add the olive oil. Once hot, add the chopped onions, minced garlic and minced ginger. Sauté for 1 minutes, stirring frequently.

2) Add the tomato paste along with ¼ cup of water. Give a good stir.

3) Stir in all the seasonings and give another good stir.

4) Stir in the coconut milk, the remainder of the water and lamb pieces. Cover and cook for 15 minutes on high pressure. When done, release the pressure naturally and remove the lid.

5) Serve and enjoy!

# 17_SALMON WITH SAUCE

**Preparation Time:** 5 minutes
**Cooking Time:** 15 minutes
**Servings:** 2

## Nutrition:

Calories 449

Total Fat 34.5g

Saturated Fat 14.4g

Cholesterol 136mg

Sodium 168mg

Total Carbohydrate 1.1g

Dietary Fiber 0.1g

Total Sugars 0g

Protein 35.2g

## INGREDIENTS:

- SALMON FILLET - **1 1/2** LB.
- DUCK FAT - **1** TBSP
- DRIED DILL WEED - ¾ TO **1** TSP
- DRIED TARRAGON - ¾ TO **1** TSP
- SALT AND PEPPER TO TASTE
- CREAM SAUCE:
- HEAVY CREAM - **1/4** CUP
- BUTTER - **2** TBSP
- DRIED DILL WEED - **1/2** TSP
- DRIED TARRAGON - **1/2** TSP
- SALT AND PEPPER TO TASTE

## DIRECTIONS:

1) Slice the salmon in half and make 2 fillets. Season skin side with salt and pepper and meat of the fish with spices.

2) In a skillet, heat 1 tbsp duck fat over medium heat.

3) Add salmon to the hot pan, skin side down.

4) Cook the salmon for about 5 minutes. When the skin is crisp, lower the heat and flip salmon.

5) Cook salmon on low heat for 7 to 15 minutes or until your desired doneness is reached.

6) Remove salmon from the pan and set aside.

7) Add spices and butter to the pan and let brown. Once browned, add cream and mix.

8) Top salmon with sauce and serve.

# 18_BUTTER CHICKEN

**Preparation Time:** 5 minutes
**Cooking Time:** 30 minutes
**Servings: 4**

## Nutrition:

Calories 414

Total Fat 32.9g

Saturated Fat 13.6g

Cholesterol 149mg

Sodium 786mg

Total Carbohydrate 2g

Dietary Fiber 0.5g

Total Sugars 0.8g

Protein 26.5g

## INGREDIENTS:

- BUTTER – ¼ CUP
- MUSHROOMS – 2 CUPS, SLICED
- CHICKEN THIGHS – 4 LARGE
- ONION POWDER – ½ TSP
- GARLIC POWDER – ½ TSP
- KOSHER SALT – 1 TSP
- BLACK PEPPER – ¼ TSP
- WATER – ½ CUP
- DIJON MUSTARD – 1 TSP
- FRESH TARRAGON – 1 TBSP, CHOPPED

## DIRECTIONS:

1) Season the chicken thighs with onion powder, garlic powder, salt, and pepper.

2) In a sauté pan, melt 1 tbsp butter.

3) Sear the chicken thighs about 3 to 4 minutes per side, or until both sides are golden brown. Remove the thighs from the pan.

4) Add the remaining 3 tbsp of butter to the pan and melt.

5) Add the mushrooms and cook for 4 to 5 minutes or until golden brown. Stirring as little as possible.

6) Add the Dijon mustard and water to the pan. Stir to deglaze.

7) Place the chicken thighs back in the pan with the skin side up.

8) Cover and simmer for 15 minutes.

9) Stir in the fresh herbs. Let sit for 5 minutes and serve.

# 19_LAMB CURRY

**Preparation Time:** 10 minutes
**Cooking Time:** 4 hours
**Servings: 6**

## Nutrition:

Calories 186,  Fat 7.2g, Saturated Fat 2.5g , Cholesterol 38mg,
Sodium 477mg, Total Carbohydrate 16.3g, Dietary Fiber 5g, Sugars
5g, Protein 14.4g

## INGREDIENTS:

- FRESH GINGER – 2 TBSP GRATED
- GARLIC – 2 CLOVES, PEELED AND MINCED
- CARDAMOM – 2 TSP
- ONION – 1 PEELED AND HOPPED
- CLOVES – 6
- LAMB MEAT – 1 POUND, CUBED
- CUMIN POWDER – 2 TSP
- GARAM MASALA – 1 TSP
- CHILI POWDER – ½ TSP
- TURMERIC – 1 TSP
- CORIANDER – 2 TSP
- SPINACH – 1 POUND
- CANNED DICED TOMATOES – 14 OUNCES

## DIRECTIONS:

1) In a slow cooker, mix lamb with tomatoes, spinach, ginger, garlic, onion, cardamom, cloves, cumin, garam masala, chili, turmeric, and coriander.

2) Stir well. Cover and cook on high for 4 hours.

3) Uncover slow cooker, stir the chili, divide into bowls, and serve.

# Chapter 5

## DINNER

# 20_BEEF & BARLEY SOUP

**Preparation Time:** 20 minutes
**Cooking Time:** 2hours 35 minutes
**Servings: 8**

## INGREDIENTS:

- 1 LB. BEEF STEW MEAT, CUT INTO 1-INCH CUBES
- 1 TBSP. CANOLA OIL
- 6 CUPS WATER
- 1 CAN (8 OZ.) TOMATO SAUCE
- 1 MEDIUM ONION, CHOPPED
- 1-1/2 TSPS. SALT
- 3/4 TSP. DRIED OREGANO
- 1/4 TSP. PEPPER
- BARLEY

## DIRECTIONS:

1) Brown beef in oil in an oven; let drain. Next, oregano, salt, onion, tomato sauce, barley, and water.

2) Bring to a boil, then reduce the heat; cover and simmer for 2 hours.

## Nutrition:

Calories: 155; Carbohydrates: 12g, Protein: 13g , Fat: 5g, Sugar: 1.6g , Sodium: 342mg, Fiber: 1g

# 21_SHRIMP SALAD

**Preparation Time:** 20 minutes
**Cooking Time:** 30 minutes
**Servings:** 4

## Nutrition:

Calories: 218; Carbohydrates: 15g  Protein: 20g  Fat: 9g  Sugar: 0.8g, Sodium: 706mg  Fiber: 2g

## INGREDIENTS:

- **1** SMALL ONION, HALVED AND THINLY SLICED
- **1/4** CUP MINCED FRESH CILANTRO
- **1** JALAPENO PEPPER, SEEDED AND CHOPPED
- **2** TBSPS. CANOLA OIL
- **2** TSPS. CHILI POWDER
- **1/2** TSP. GROUND CUMIN
- **1/2** TSP. GROUND CORIANDER
- **1/2** TSP. PEPPER
- **1/4** TSP. SALT
- **1** LB. UNCOOKED MEDIUM SHRIMP, PEELED AND DEVEINED
- **6** CUPS TORN LEAF LETTUCE
- **1/2** CUP FAT-FREE RANCH SALAD DRESSING

## DIRECTIONS:

1) Mix the first 9 ingredients together in a zip lock plastic bag then put in the shrimp. Seal the zip lock bag and turn to coat the shrimp. Keep in the fridge for 30 minutes.
2) Insert the drained marinated shrimps onto 4 soaked wooden or metal skewers. Use tongs to lightly rub an oiled paper towel on the grill rack.
3) Put the shrimp skewers on the grill over medium heat then cover or broil the shrimp 4 inches from heat for 3 to 4 minutes per side or until the shrimp turn pink in color.
4) Place lettuce on a plate and put grilled shrimps on top, this recipe makes 4 plates. Serve right away with the dressing.

# 22_Garlic Mushroom Frittata

**Preparation Time:** 30 minutes
**Cooking Time:** 10 to 30 minutes
**Servings: 2**

## Ingredients:

- LOW-CALORIE COOKING SPRAY
- 250G/9OZ CHESTNUT MUSHROOMS, SLICED
- 1 SMALL GARLIC CLOVE, CRUSHED
- 1 TBSP THINLY SLICED FRESH CHIVES
- 4 LARGE FREE-RANGE EGGS, BEATEN
- FRESHLY GROUND BLACK PEPPER
- FOR THE SALAD:
- 1 LITTLE GEM LETTUCE, LEAVES SEPARATED
- 100G/3½OZ CHERRY TOMATOES, HALVED
- 1/3 CUCUMBER, CUT INTO CHUNKS

# Directions

1) Spray a small, flame-proof frying pan with oil and place over a high heat. (The base of the pan shouldn't be wider than about 18cm/7in.) Stir-fry the mushrooms in three batches for 2-3 minutes, or until softened and lightly browned. Tip the cooked mushrooms into a sieve over a bowl to catch any juices – you don't want the mushrooms to become soggy.

2) Return all the mushrooms to the pan and stir in the garlic and chives, and a pinch of ground black pepper. Cook for a further minute, then reduce the heat to low.

3) Preheat the grill to its hottest setting. Pour the eggs over the mushrooms. Cook for five minutes, or until almost set.

4) Place the pan under the grill for 3-4 minutes, or until set.

5) Combine the salad ingredients in a bowl.

6) Remove from the grill and loosen the sides of the frittata with a round-bladed knife. Turn out onto a board and cut into wedges. Serve hot or cold with the salad.

## Nutrition:

Calories 243

Protein 14g

Carbohydrate 3.5g

Fat 14g

Fiber 2.5g

# 23_BROCCOLI SALAD

**Preparation Time:** 5 minutes
**Cooking Time:** 0 minutes
**Servings: 4**

## INGREDIENTS:

- 2 CUPS FRESH, BROCCOLI FLORETS
- 1/2 CUP ZESTY ITALIAN DRESSING
- 1 RED ONION, SLICED IN RINGS
- 1/4 CUP SUNFLOWER SEEDS

## DIRECTIONS:

1) Combine the broccoli, Italian dressing and onions in a large bowl.
2) Toss to coat salad evenly and refrigerate for 1 hour.
3) Garnish with sunflower seeds before serving.

## Nutrition:

Calories: 200;
Carbohydrates: 1.5g
Protein: 11g
Fat: 3g
Sugar: 0g
Sodium: 389mg
Fiber: 0.4g

# 24_LAMB CHOPS IN MINT CREAM SAUCE

**Preparation Time:** 15 minutes
**Cooking Time:** 40 minutes
**Servings:** 4

## Nutrition:

Calories: 693; Carbohydrates: 0.2g Protein: 12g Fat:33.8g Sugar: 3g Sodium: 809mg Fiber: 2g

## INGREDIENTS:

- **4** LAMB CHOPS
- **2** TABLESPOONS OF EXTRA-VIRGIN OLIVE OIL
- **1** CUP OF HOMEMADE LOW-SODIUM BEEF BROTH
- **2** TABLESPOONS OF FRESH DILL, CHOPPED
- **¼** CUP OF FRESH MINT, CHOPPED
- **1** TABLESPOON OF FRESHLY SQUEEZED LEMON JUICE
- **2** TABLESPOONS OF HEAVY WHIPPING CREAM
- FINE SEA SALT AND FRESHLY CRACKED BLACK PEPPER (TO TASTE)

## DIRECTIONS:

1) Season the lamb ribs with sea salt and freshly cracked black pepper.

2) Press the "Sauté" setting on your Instant Pot and add the olive oil. Once hot, add the lamb ribs and sear for 3 minutes or until brown.

3) Pour in the beef broth. Lock the lid and cook at high pressure for 30 minutes. When the cooking is done, naturally release the pressure for 10 minutes, then quick release the remaining pressure. Carefully remove the lid.

4) In a blender, add the fresh dill, mint, lemon juice, heavy whipping cream. Blend until smooth.

5) Transfer the lamb chops to serving plates and top with the mint cream sauce.

# 25_SOUTHWEST CHICKEN SALAD

**Preparation Time:** 5 minutes
**Cooking Time:** 0 minutes
**Servings:** 4

## INGREDIENTS:

- **2** CUPS COOKED, DICED CHICKEN
- **1/2** CUP FINELY CHOPPED CELERY
- **1/4** CUP FRENCH DRESSING
- **1/4** CUP MAYONNAISE OR SALAD DRESSING
- **1/8** TEASPOON CAYENNE PEPPER

## DIRECTIONS:

1) Mix all the ingredients together and serve on a bed of lettuce.

2) Makes 3-4 servings.

3) Serve and enjoy.

## Nutrition:

Calories: 243;

Carbohydrates: 3g

Protein: 19g

Fat: 4g

Sugar: 0.6g

Sodium: 289mg

Fiber: 0.7g

# 26_CHICKEN SALAD

**Preparation Time:** 5 minutes
**Cooking Time:** 0 minutes
**Servings: 4**

## Nutrition:

Calories: 190; Carbohydrates: 2.5g Protein: 1.9g Fat: 5g Sugar: 1.6g Sodium: 476mg Fiber: 3.7g

## Ingredients:

- Escarole, canons or watercress
- Grilled chicken
- Pistachios
- Sweet onion (rings)
- Pink pepper
- Pink salt
- Extra virgin olive oil 3 tablespoons
- 1 teaspoon Dijon mustard in grain
- 1 teaspoon honey

## Directions:

1) Clean and cut delicious escarole or any other green leafy vegetable such as canons, and watercress.
2) Add chopped pistachios.
3) You can use any other dried fruit that you like more or that you have in the pantry: pine nuts, pecans, almonds.
4) Peel and chop onion, which gives it a spicy point always.
5) And if you dare with the vinaigrette mix, a teaspoon of Dijon mustard in grain, a teaspoon of honey, extra virgin olive oil, lime juice and salt, and pink pepper.
6) Pink pepper is an ingredient that gives an extraordinary touch, in my opinion, and you can crush some and others you leave them whole.
7) The so-called pink pepper, in reality, is the grain of a Brazilian pepper shaker. Its flavor is very peculiar, the mixture of sweet, citrus, little spicy flavor, reminiscent of pine.
8) Finally, you add the roast chicken that you can buy well packed or remains of some homemade preparation.

# 27_TUSCAN CHICKEN SAUTÉ

**Preparation Time:** 10 minutes
**Cooking Time:** 35 minutes
**Servings: 4**

## Nutrition:

Calories: 483 fat: 38g Total carbs: 5g Fiber: 1g; Net carbs: 3g
Sodium: 332mg Protein: 31g

# Ingredients:

- **1**-POUND BONELESS CHICKEN BREASTS, EACH CUT INTO THREE PIECES
- SEA SALT, FOR SEASONING
- FRESHLY GROUND BLACK PEPPER, FOR SEASONING
- **3** TABLESPOONS OLIVE OIL
- **1** TABLESPOON MINCED GARLIC
- ¾ CUP CHICKEN STOCK
- **1** TEASPOON DRIED OREGANO
- ½ TEASPOON DRIED BASIL
- ½ CUP HEAVY (WHIPPING) CREAM
- ½ CUP SHREDDED ASIAGO CHEESE
- **1** CUP FRESH SPINACH
- ¼ CUP SLICED KALAMATA OLIVES

# Directions:

1) Prepare the chicken. Pat, the chicken, breasts dry and lightly season them with salt and pepper.
2) Sauté the chicken. In a large skillet over medium-high heat, warm the olive oil. Add the chicken and sauté until it is golden brown and just cooked through, about 15 minutes in total. Transfer the chicken to a plate and set it aside.
3) Make the sauce. Put the garlic to the skillet, then sauté until it's softened about 2 minutes. Stir in the chicken stock, oregano, and basil, scraping up any browned bits in the skillet. Bring to a boil, then reduce the heat to low and simmer until the sauce is reduced by about one-quarter, about 10 minutes.
4) Finish the dish. Stir in the cream, Asiago, and simmer, stirring the sauce frequently, until it has thickened about 5 minutes. Put back the chicken to the skillet along with any accumulated juices. Stir in the spinach and olives and simmer until the spinach is wilted about 2 minutes.
5) Serve. Divide the chicken and sauce between four plates and serve it immediately.

# 28_BREADED CHICKEN FILLETS

**Preparation Time:** 5 minutes
**Cooking Time:** 10-25 minutes
**Servings: 4**

## Nutrition:

Calories 367
Fat 16.9g
Carbs 6g
Protein 43g
Fiber 0.7g

## INGREDIENTS:

- **1** POUND CHICKEN FILLETS
- **3** BELL PEPPERS, QUARTERED LENGTHWISE
- **1/3** CUP ROMANO CHEESE
- **2** TEASPOONS OLIVE OIL
- **1** GARLIC CLOVE, MINCED
- KOSHER SALT, TO TASTE
- GROUND BLACK PEPPER, TO TASTE
- **1/3** CUP CRUSHED PORK RINDS

## DIRECTIONS:

1) Set oven to 410°F

2) Mix the crushed pork rinds, Romano cheese, olive oil, and minced garlic. Dredge the chicken into this mixture.

3) Bring the chicken into a lightly greased baking sheet. Sprinkle with salt and black pepper to taste.

4) Scatter the peppers around the chicken and bake in the preheated oven for 20 to 25 minutes or until thoroughly cooked.

# 29_Mexican-Braised Pork with Sweet Potatoes

**Preparation Time:** 10 minutes
**Cooking Time:** 25 minutes
**Servings: 4**

## Ingredients:

- **3** POUNDS PORK LOIN
- **2** PEELED AND DICED SWEET POTATOES
- **1** CUP TOMATO SALSA
- **½** CUP CHICKEN STOCK
- **1/3** CUP MEXICAN SPICE BLEND

## Directions:

1) Season the pork all over with the spice blend.
2) Turn your cooker to "chicken/meat" and heat.
3) When hot, sear the pork on both sides. If the meat sticks, pour in a little chicken stock.
4) When the pork is golden, pour in stock and salsa.
5) Tumble sweet potatoes on one side of the pot and seal the lid.
6) Adjust time to 25 minutes.
7) When the timer beeps, hit "cancel" and wait 10 minutes before quick-releasing.
8) The pork should be cooked to 145-degrees, and the potatoes should be tender.
9) Remove the pork and rest 8-10 minutes before serving.

## Nutrition:

Total calories: 513, Protein: 73, Carbs: 17, Fat: 14 Fiber: 1

# Chapter 6

## SNACKS

# 30_BUFFALO CAULIFLOWER

**Preparation Time:** 10 minutes
**Cooking Time:** 25 minutes
**Servings: 4**

## INGREDIENTS:

- **4 CUPS CAULIFLOWER FLORETS**
- **4 TABLESPOONS SALTED GRASS-FED BUTTER**
- **¼ CUP HOT SAUCE**
- **1 GARLIC CLOVE, MINCED**
- **¼ TSP. PAPRIKA**
- **¼ TSP. SEA SALT**
- **¼ TSP. CAYENNE PEPPER**
- **FRESHLY GROUND BLACK PEPPER**
- **BLUE CHEESE DRESSING, FOR SERVING (OPTIONAL)**

## DIRECTIONS:

1) Set the oven to 375°F.
2) Take the cauliflower florets in a large baking dish.
3) In a small microwave-safe bowl, combine together the the butter, hot sauce, garlic, paprika, salt, cayenne pepper, and black pepper. Microwave for at least 30 seconds, stir the mixture, and continue microwaving and stirring the sauce in 15-second intervals until it is smooth and creamy.
4) Put the sauce over the cauliflower then toss to coat the florets evenly. Bake for at least 25 minutes.
5) Serve the cauliflower warm with a small bowl of blue cheese dressing for dipping (optionally)

## Nutrition:

Calories: 130, Fat: 12g, Saturated Fat: 7g, Protein: 2g, Cholesterol: 31mg, Carbohydrates: 6g, Fiber: 3g, Net Carbs: 3g

# 31_ROASTED BRUSSELS SPROUTS WITH PECANS AND GORGONZOLA

**Preparation Time:** 10 minutes
**Cooking Time:** 35 minutes
**Servings: 4**

## Nutrition:

Calories: 149, Fat: 11 g, Carbohydrates: 10 g, Fiber: 4 g, Protein: 5g

## INGREDIENTS:

- BRUSSELS SPROUTS, FRESH- 1 POUND
- PECANS, CHOPPED- ¼ CUP
- OLIVE OIL- 1 TABLESPOON
- EXTRA OLIVE OIL TO OIL THE BAKING TRAY
- PEPPER AND SALT FOR TASTING
- GORGONZOLA CHEESE- ¼ CUP (IF YOU PREFER NOT TO USE THE GORGONZOLA CHEESE, YOU CAN TOSS THE BRUSSELS SPROUTS WHEN HOT, WITH 2 TABLESPOONS OF BUTTER INSTEAD.

## DIRECTIONS:

1) Warm the oven to 350 degrees Fahrenheit or 175 Celsius.
2) Rub a large pan or any vessel you wish to use with a little bit of olive oil. You can use a paper towel or a pastry brush.
3) Cut off the ends of the Brussels sprouts if you need to and then cut then in a lengthwise direction into halves. (Fear not if a few of the leaves come off of them, some may become deliciously crunchy during cooking)
4) Chop up all of the pecans using a knife and then measure them for the amount.
5) Put your Brussels sprouts as well as the sliced pecans inside a bowl, and cover them all with some olive oil, pepper, and salt (be generous).
6) Arrange all of your pecans and Brussels sprouts onto your roasting pan in a single layer
7) Roast this for 30 to 35 minutes, or when they become tender and can be pierced with a fork easily. Stir during cooking if you wish to get a more even browning.
8) Once cooked, toss them with the Gorgonzola Cheese (or butter) before you serve them. Serve them hot.

# 32_Eggplant Fries

**Preparation Time** 10 minutes
**Cooking Time:** 15 minutes
**Servings: 8**

## Nutrition:

Calories: 212,

Fat: 15.8g,

Carbohydrates: 12.1 g,

Protein: 8.6 g

## INGREDIENTS:

- 2 EGGS
- 2 CUPS ALMOND FLOUR
- 2 TABLESPOONS COCONUT OIL, SPRAY
- 2 EGGPLANT, PEELED AND CUT THINLY
- SALT AND PEPPER

## DIRECTIONS:

1) Preheat your oven to 400 degrees Fahrenheit
2) Take a bowl and mix with salt and black pepper in it
3) Take another bowl and beat eggs until frothy
4) Dip the eggplant pieces into eggs
5) Then coat them with flour mixture
6) Add another layer of flour and egg
7) Then, take a baking sheet and grease with coconut oil on top
8) Bake for about 15 minutes
9) Serve and enjoy.

# 33_STUFFED BEEF LOIN IN STICKY SAUCE

**Preparation Time:** 15 minutes
**Cooking Time:** 6 minutes
**Servings: 4**

## Nutrition:

Calories: 321, Protein: 18.35 g,  Fat: 26.68 g,  Carbohydrates: 2.75 g

## INGREDIENTS:

- 1 TABLESPOON ERYTHRITOL
- 1 TABLESPOON LEMON JUICE

- 4 TABLESPOONS WATER
- 1 TABLESPOON BUTTER
- ½ TEASPOON TOMATO SAUCE
- ¼ TEASPOON DRIED ROSEMARY
- 9 OUNCES BEEF LOIN
- 3 OUNCES CELERY ROOT, GRATED

- 3 OUNCES BACON, SLICED
- 1 TABLESPOON WALNUTS, CHOPPED
- ¾ TEASPOON GARLIC, DICED
- 2 TEASPOONS BUTTER
- 1 TABLESPOON OLIVE OIL
- 1 TEASPOON SALT
- ½ CUP OF WATER

## DIRECTIONS:

1) Cut the beef loin into the layer and spread it with the dried rosemary, butter, and salt.

2) Then place over the beef loin: grated celery root, sliced bacon, walnuts, and diced garlic. Roll the beef loin and brush it with olive oil.

3) Secure the meat with the help of the toothpicks.

4) Place it in the tray and add a ½ cup of water. Cook the meat in the preheated to 365F oven for 40 minutes.

5) Meanwhile, make the sticky sauce: mix up together Erythritol, lemon juice, 4 tablespoons of water, and butter.

6) Preheat the mixture until it starts to boil.

7) Then add tomato sauce and whisk it well.

8) Bring the sauce to boil and remove from the heat. When the beef loin is cooked, remove it from the oven and brush with the cooked sticky sauce very generously.

9) Slice the beef roll and sprinkle with the remaining sauce.

# 34_Parmesan Crisps

**Preparation Time** 5 minutes
**Cooking Time:** 25 minutes
**Servings: 8**

## Ingredients:

- **1** TEASPOON BUTTER
- **8** OUNCES PARMESAN CHEESE, FULL FAT AND SHREDDED

## Directions:

1) Preheat your oven to 400 degrees F
2) Put parchment paper on a baking sheet and grease with butter
3) Spoon parmesan into 8 mounds, spreading them apart evenly
4) Flatten them
5) Bake for 5 minutes until browned
6) Let them cool
7) Serve and enjoy.

## Nutrition:

Calories: 133,

Fat: 11 g,

Carbohydrates: 1 g,

Protein: 11 g

# 35_ARTICHOKE PETALS BITES

**Preparation Time**: 10 minutes
**Cooking Time:** 10 minutes
**Servings: 8**

## INGREDIENTS:

- 8 OUNCES ARTICHOKE PETALS, BOILED, DRAINED, WITHOUT SALT
- ½ CUP ALMOND FLOUR
- 4 OUNCES PARMESAN, GRATED
- 2 TABLESPOONS ALMOND BUTTER, MELTED

## DIRECTIONS:

1) In the mixing bowl, mix up together almond flour and grated Parmesan.
2) Preheat the oven to 355F.
3) Dip the artichoke petals in the almond butter and then coat in the almond flour mixture.
4) Place them in the tray.
5) Transfer the tray in the preheated oven and cook the petals for 10 minutes.
6) Chill the cooked petal bites little before serving.

## Nutrition:

Calories: 93,

Protein: 6.54 g,

Fat: 3.72 g,

Carbohydrates: 9.08 g

# 36_ROASTED BROCCOLI

**Preparation Time** 5 minutes
**Cooking Time:** 20 minutes
**Servings: 4**

## INGREDIENTS:

- **4 CUPS BROCCOLI FLORETS**
- **1 TABLESPOON OLIVE OIL**
- **SALT AND PEPPER TO TASTE**

## DIRECTIONS:

1) Preheat your oven to 400 degrees F
2) Add broccoli in a zip bag alongside oil and shake until coated
3) Add seasoning and shake again
4) Spread broccoli out on the baking sheet, bake for 20 minutes
5) Let it cool and serve.

## Nutrition:

Calories: 62,

Fat: 4 g,

Carbohydrates: 4 g,

Protein: 4 g

# Chapter 7

## DESSERTS

# 37_Chocolate Truffles

**Preparation Time:** 10 minutes
**Cooking Time:** 60 minutes
**Servings: 12**

## Ingredients:

- Ripe Hass avocados – 2 pitted and skinned
- Coconut oil – 2 tbsp
- Premium cocoa powder – ½ cup
- Granulated sugar substitute – 1 tbsp
- Sugar free chocolate-flavored syrup – 2 tbsp
- Heavy whipping cream – 2 tbsp
- Bourbon – 2 tbsp
- Chopped pecans – ½ cup

## Directions:

1) Combine all ingredients except pecans in a small blender and process until smooth. Chill for 1 hour.
2) Make 1-inch balls and then roll in the pecans.
3) Chill in the refrigerator.

## Nutrition:

Calories 124, Fat 11.7g, Saturated Fat 4g, Cholesterol 3mg
Sodium 9mg, Carbohydrate 4.5g, Dietary Fiber 2.9g, Total Sugars 0.4g, Protein 1.8g

# 38_LOW-CARB BROWNIES

**Preparation Time:** 10 minutes
**Cooking Time:** 20 minutes
**Servings: 16**

## INGREDIENTS:

- **7** TABLESPOONS COCONUT OIL, MELTED
- **6** TABLESPOONS PLANT-BASED SWEETENER
- **1** LARGE EGG
- **2** EGG YOLK
- **1/2** TSP MINT EXTRACT
- **5** OUNCES SUGAR-FREE DARK CHOCOLATE
- **¼** CUP PLANT-BASED CHOCOLATE PROTEIN POWDER
- **1** TSP BAKING SODA
- **¼** TSP SEA SALT
- **2** TABLESPOONS VANILLA ALMOND MILK, UNSWEETENED

## DIRECTIONS:

1) Start by preheating the oven to 350°F and then take an 8x8 inch pan and line it with parchment paper, being sure to leave some extra sticking up to use later to help you get them out of the pan after they are cooked.

2) Into a medium-sized vessel, use a hand mixer, and blend 5 Tablespoons of the coconut oil (save the rest for later), as well as the egg, Erythritol, egg yolks, and the mint extract all together for 1 minute. After this minute, the mixture will become a lighter yellow hue.

3) Take 4 oz of the chocolate and put it in a (microwave-safe) bowl, as well as with the other 2 Tablespoons of melted coconut oil.

4) Cook this chocolate and oil mixture on half power, at 30-second intervals, being sure to stir at each interval, just until the chocolate becomes melted and smooth

5) While the egg mixture is being beaten, add in the melted chocolate mixture into the egg mixture until this becomes thick and homogenous.

6) Add in your protein powder of choice, salt, baking soda, and stir until homogenous. Then, vigorously whisk your almond milk in until the batter becomes a bit smoother.

7) Finely chop the rest of your chocolate and stir these bits of chocolate into the batter you have made.

8) Spread the batter evenly into the pan you have prepared, and bake this until the edges of the batter just begin to become darker, and the center of the batter rises a little bit. You can also tell by sliding a toothpick into the middle, and when it comes out clean, it is ready. This will take approximately 20 to 21 minutes. Be sure that you do NOT over bake them!

9) Let them cool in the pan they cooked in for about 20 minutes. Then, carefully use the excess paper handles to take the brownies out of the pan and put them onto a wire cooling rack.

10) Make sure that they cool completely, and when they do, cut them, and they are ready to eat!

## Nutrition:

Calories 107, Fats 10g, Carbohydrates 5.7g, Protein 2.5g

# 39_BLUEBERRY CAKE

**Preparation Time:** 10 minutes
**Cooking Time:** 40 minutes
**Servings: 4**

## INGREDIENTS:

- ALMOND FLOUR - 2/3 CUP
- EGGS – 5
- ALMOND MILK – 1/3 CUP
- ERYTHRITOL – ¼ CUP
- VANILLA EXTRACT – 2 TSP
- JUICE OF 2 LEMONS
- LEMON ZEST – 1 TSP
- BAKING SODA – ½ TSP
- PINCH OF SALT

- **FRESH BLUEBERRIES** – ½ CUP
- **BUTTER** – 1 TO 2 TBSP MELTED

## FOR THE FROSTING:

- **HEAVY CREAM** – ½ CUP
- **JUICE OF 1 LEMON**
- **ERYTHRITOL** – 1/8 CUP

## DIRECTIONS:

1) Preheat the oven to 350°F.
2) In a bowl, add the almond flour, eggs, and almond milk and mix well until smooth.
3) Then add the erythritol, a pinch of salt, baking soda, lemon zest, lemon juice, and vanilla extract. Mix and combine well.
4) Fold in the blueberries.
5) Use the butter to grease the spring form pans.
6) Pour the batter into the two greased pans.
7) Place on a baking sheet for even baking.
8) Place in the oven to bake until cooked through in the middle and slightly brown on the top about 35 to 40 minutes.
9) Allow to cool before removing from the pan.
10) Mix together the erythritol, lemon juice, heavy cream for the frosting. Mix well.
11) Pour frosting on top and spread. Serve.

## Nutrition:

Calories 272, Fat 23.8g, Cholesterol 240mg, Sodium 287mg

Carbohydrate 21g, Dietary Fiber 1.4g, Sugars 18.2g, Protein 8.9g

# 40_Apple Bread

**Preparation Time:** 10 minutes
**Cooking Time:** 20 minutes
**Servings: 10**

## Nutrition:

Calories 210,

Carbohydrates 41g,

Fats 5g,

Protein 5g

## Ingredients:

- ½ CUP HONEY
- ½ TSP. NUTMEG
- ½ TSP. SALT
- 1 CUP APPLESAUCE, SWEETENED
- 1 TSP. BAKING SODA
- 1 TSP. VANILLA EXTRACT

- 2 ¼ CUP WHOLE WHEAT FLOUR
- 2 LARGE EGGS
- 2 TBSP. VEGETABLE OIL
- 2 TSP. BAKING POWDER
- 2 TSP. CINNAMON
- 4 CUP APPLES, DICED

## Directions:

1) Preheat oven to 375° Fahrenheit and oil a loaf pan with non-stick spray or your choice of oil.
2) Beat eggs in a mixing bowl and stir until completely smooth.
3) Add the honey, oil, applesauce, cinnamon, vanilla, nutmeg, baking powder, baking soda, and salt. Whisk until completely combined and smooth.
4) Add the flour into the bowl and whisk to combine, making sure not to over-mix. Simply stir it enough to incorporate the flour.
5) Add apples to the batter and mix once more to combine.
6) Pour the batter into the loaf pan and smooth the top with your spatula.
7) Bake for 60 minutes, or until an inserted toothpick in the center comes out clean.
8) Let stand for 10 minutes, and then transfer the loaf to a cooling rack to cool completely.
9) Slice into 10 pieces and serve!

# 41_Coconut Protein Balls

**Preparation Time**: 10 minutes
**Cooking Time:** 15 minutes
**Servings: 4**

## Ingredients:

- ¼ CUP VEGAN VANILLA PROTEIN POWDER
- ¼ CUP HEMP SEEDS
- ¼ CUP COCONUT BUTTER
- 1 TABLESPOON MAPLE SYRUP
- 1 TABLESPOON WATER
- 1 TEASPOON CINNAMON

## Directions:

1) Pulse all the ingredients in a mini chopper food processor and until combined.

2) Stir the dough and roll the mixture into small ball using your hands. You should get about 8 balls. Add some drops of water if the dough is very dry.

3) Eat immediately. You can alternatively store in an airtight container for about 4 days at room temperature or up to 2 weeks in the refrigerator or up 3 months in a freezer.

## Nutrition:

Calories 234, Carbohydrates 5g , Protein 16g, Fats 5g

# 42_SUNFLOWER COOKIES

**Preparation Time:** 2 minutes
**Cooking Time:** 8 minutes
**Servings: 2**

## Nutrition:

Calories: 70, Protein: 3 g, Carbs: 65 g, Fat: 6 g

## INGREDIENTS:

- **1** EGG
- **½** CUP OF SUNFLOWER SEED BUTTER
- **1** TABLESPOON OF COCONUT OIL
- **1** TABLESPOON OF TRUVIA
- **½** TSP OF VANILLA EXTRACT
- **¼** TSP OF BAKING POWDER
- **¼** TSP OF BAKING SODA
- **¼** TSP OF SALT

## DIRECTIONS:

1) Set your oven for 360 degrees, and get out a slightly greased cookie sheet.

2) While your oven heats up, deposit your egg into your mixing bowl followed by your ½ cup of sunflower seed butter, your tablespoon of coconut oil, your tablespoon of Truvia, your ½ tsp of vanilla extract, your ¼ tsp of baking powder, your ¼ tsp of baking soda, and your ¼ tsp of salt.

3) Stir all of your ingredients together well before using your (clean) hands to form 8 individual clumps out of the mixture.

4) Arrange your clumps evenly on your greased cooking sheet and place the sheet into the oven.

5) Allow to cook for about 8 minutes or until golden brown.

6) Take out of oven and allow cooling.

7) Serve when ready.

# 43_Chocolate Chia Pudding

**Preparation Time:** 3 minutes
**Cooking Time**: 0 minutes
**Servings: 1**

## Ingredients:

- ¾ CUP MILK, UNSWEETENED
- 2 TSP. HONEY
- 1 TSP. VANILLA EXTRACT
- 4 TBSP. CHIA SEEDS
- 1 TBSP. COCOA POWDER, UNSWEETENED

## Directions:

1) In a glass jar or container, combine all liquid ingredients and mix completely.
2) Add chia seeds and cocoa powder and mix completely.
3) Allow everything to sit for about 10 minutes before stirring once again, then sealing tightly and storing in the refrigerator overnight.
4) Stir well before eating and enjoy cold!

## Nutrition:

Calories 329
Carbohydrates 40g
Fats 14g
Protein 14g

# 44_PEANUT BUTTER BARS

**Preparation Time:** 6 minutes
**Cooking Time**: 8 minutes
**Servings: 2**

## INGREDIENTS:

- **1** CUP OF PEANUT BUTTER
- **½** TSP OF PURE VANILLA EXTRACT
- **¼** TSP OF SALT
- **2** TABLESPOONS OF ALMOND FLOUR
- **¼** CUP OF MILK

## DIRECTIONS:

1) Deposit your cup of peanut butter in to a mixing bowl, followed by your ½ tsp. of pure vanilla extract, your ¼ tsp. of salt, your 2 tablespoons of almond flour and your ¼ cup of milk.
2) Stir your entire ingredients together well and pour into an oven safe baking dish.
3) Place dish in oven and set temperature for 380 degrees.
4) Cook for about 8 minutes.
5) Take out of oven and allow cooling at room temperature.
6) Once cool, slice and serve.

## Nutrition:

Calories: 116, Protein: 4 g, Carbs: 6 g, Fat: 5 g

# 45_HOMEMADE DARK CHOCOLATE

**Preparation Time:** 48 minutes
**Cooking Time:** 0 minutes
**Servings: 2**

## INGREDIENTS:

- **2** TABLESPOONS OF COCONUT OIL
- **¼** CUP OF COCOA POWDER
- **2** TABLESPOONS OF HONEY
- **1** TSP OF VANILLA EXTRACT

## DIRECTIONS:

1) Deposit your 2 tablespoons of coconut oil, followed by your ¼ cup of cocoa powder, your 2 tablespoons of honey, and your tsp of vanilla extract to a mixing bowl and spend a few minutes stirring it all together well.

2) Once thoroughly mixed together, cover the bowl and place it in the fridge for about 45 minutes.

3) Once chilled and hardened your Homemade Dark Chocolate is ready to eat!

## Nutrition:

Calories: 170
Protein: 2 g
Carbs: 15 g
Fat: 3 g

# Conclusion

In anything new that we try, there is a chance that we may fall off track. Fasting or following a new diet plan are no different. The focus should not be on the fact that you fell off but on how you decide to come back and approach it again. You need not give up altogether if you have a day or two where you did not accomplish your full fast. You just need to re-examine your plan and approach it in a different way. Maybe your fasting period was too long for your first try.

Maybe you're fasting and eating windows did not match up with your sleep-wake cycle as well as they could have. Any of these factors can be adjusted to better suit your lifestyle needs and make fasting or a specific diet work for you. Being able to be flexible with yourself is something that trying a new diet regimen like this can teach you. With the human body, there is never a right or a wrong way to approach anything; there is only a multitude of different ways and some that will be better for your specific body and mind than others. Being opened to trying different variations and adjusting your plan as you go can be the difference between success and deciding to give up.

If you fall off track, scale your plan back a little bit and try it again. If you are worried that you are not doing enough, begin with the scaled back plan, and get used to this first, you can always increase your fasting times later on once you know you are completely comfortable with a shorter fasting time.

If this guidebook has taught you anything, the hope is that it has taught you how many variables are involved when it comes to health and wellness. This guidebook aimed to share with you the plethora of options that are available to you when it comes to intermittent fasting for women over 50.

Think back on the many options that were laid out for you in this guidebook involving diet options and specific foods that have the ability to induce autophagy in the brain. It is your job now to decide which of these foods or supplements to include in your life and to practice a sort of trial and error, noting which ones make you feel great and which ones you prefer to go without. With all of this information, you can decide which ways fit best with your specific lifestyle and your preferences.

As you take all of this information forth with you, it may seem overwhelming to begin applying this into your own life. Remember, life is a process, and you do not need to expect perfection from yourself. By taking the steps to read this guidebook, you are already on your way to changing your life. IF you fall off of the diet and you need inspiration, come back and review this guidebook and remind yourself why you wanted to begin it in the first place.

CPSIA information can be obtained
at www.ICGtesting.com
Printed in the USA
BVHW091404290621
610728BV00004B/1228